Inside Your Mouth

Contents

Written by Fran Drake

Introduction

Open wide.
Take a look inside your mouth.
You have different kinds of teeth.
They are different shapes and sizes.

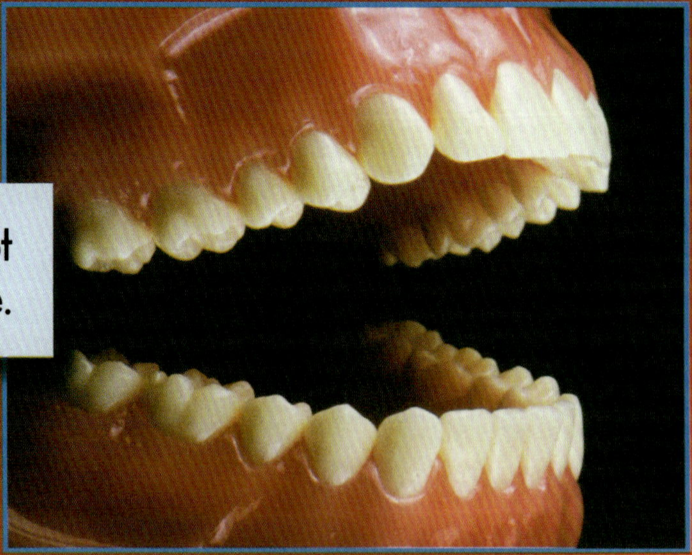

Your teeth do not all look the same.

Have you ever taken a look inside your mouth in a mirror?

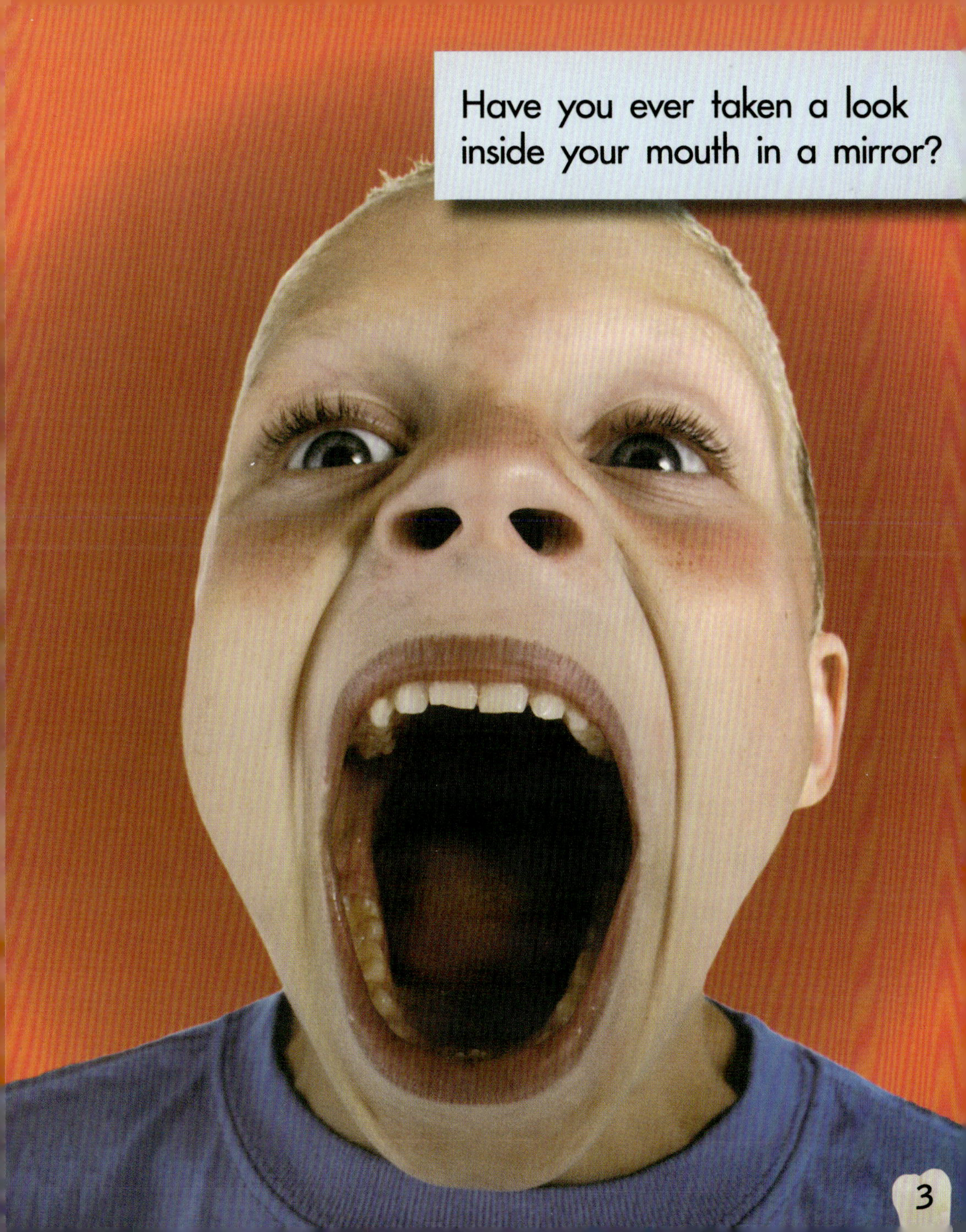

The Inside of Your Mouth

There are different parts to your mouth.
The inside is covered in soft, pink tissue.
The tissue wrapped around your teeth
is your **gums**.
The big piece of muscular tissue
in the middle of your mouth is your tongue.
Your tongue helps you taste, chew,
and swallow your food.
It also helps you speak.

Your tongue is a big piece of muscle.

Your mouth makes a thick, colourless fluid called **saliva**.
As soon as you eat or smell food, you make saliva.
Saliva makes food easier to chew and swallow.
Saliva also helps keep your teeth clean.
It kills tiny things that can make you sick, or **bacteria**, that live in your mouth.

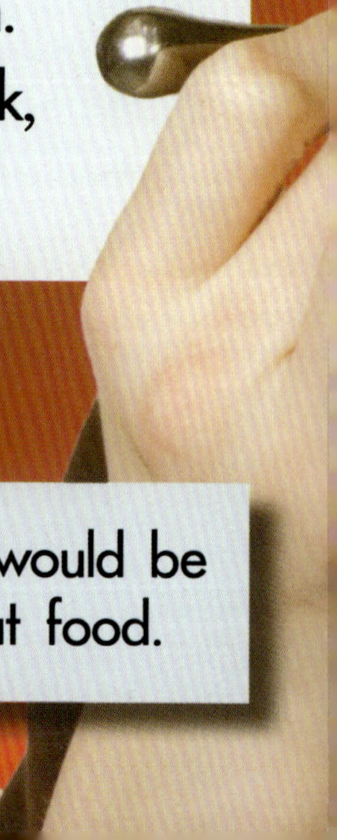

Without saliva, it would be very difficult to eat food.

Parts of a Tooth

The part of a tooth that you can see
above your gums is called the crown.
The crown has a hard outer layer
called **enamel**.
Enamel is the hardest thing in your body.

The gums protect the lower part
of the tooth, which is called the root.
The root is fixed to your jaw.
The gums and the roots
hold your teeth in place.
Each tooth has the same parts.

The crown is usually the only part of a tooth that you can see.

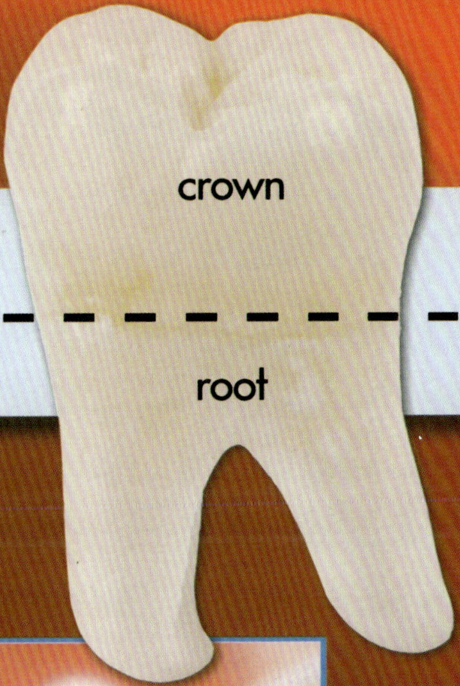

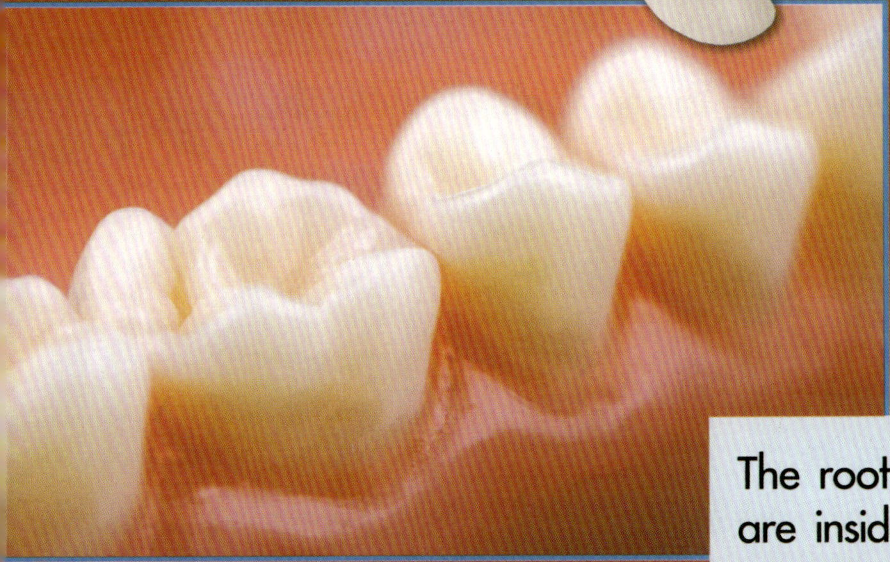

The roots of teeth are inside the gums.

Two Kinds of Teeth

The first teeth you get are baby teeth.
In their first year, babies start growing teeth.
By the time children are
two and a half years old,
they have 20 baby teeth.
These teeth last until children
are about six years old.
Then, they start losing their baby teeth.

These children have lost some of their baby teeth.

When you lose your baby teeth,
you have a funny smile for a while.

This girl has grown permanent teeth.

Then, the permanent teeth grow.
They are bigger than the baby teeth.
By the time children are 13 years old,
they have 32 permanent teeth.
Your permanent teeth should last
for the rest of your life.

What Teeth Do

Different teeth have different jobs.
The teeth that grow in the front
of your mouth are called incisors.
You use them to bite off pieces of food.
Next to the incisors are the canines.
You use them to hold or tear food.
The teeth at the back are called molars.
You use them for chewing.

Different Kinds of Teeth

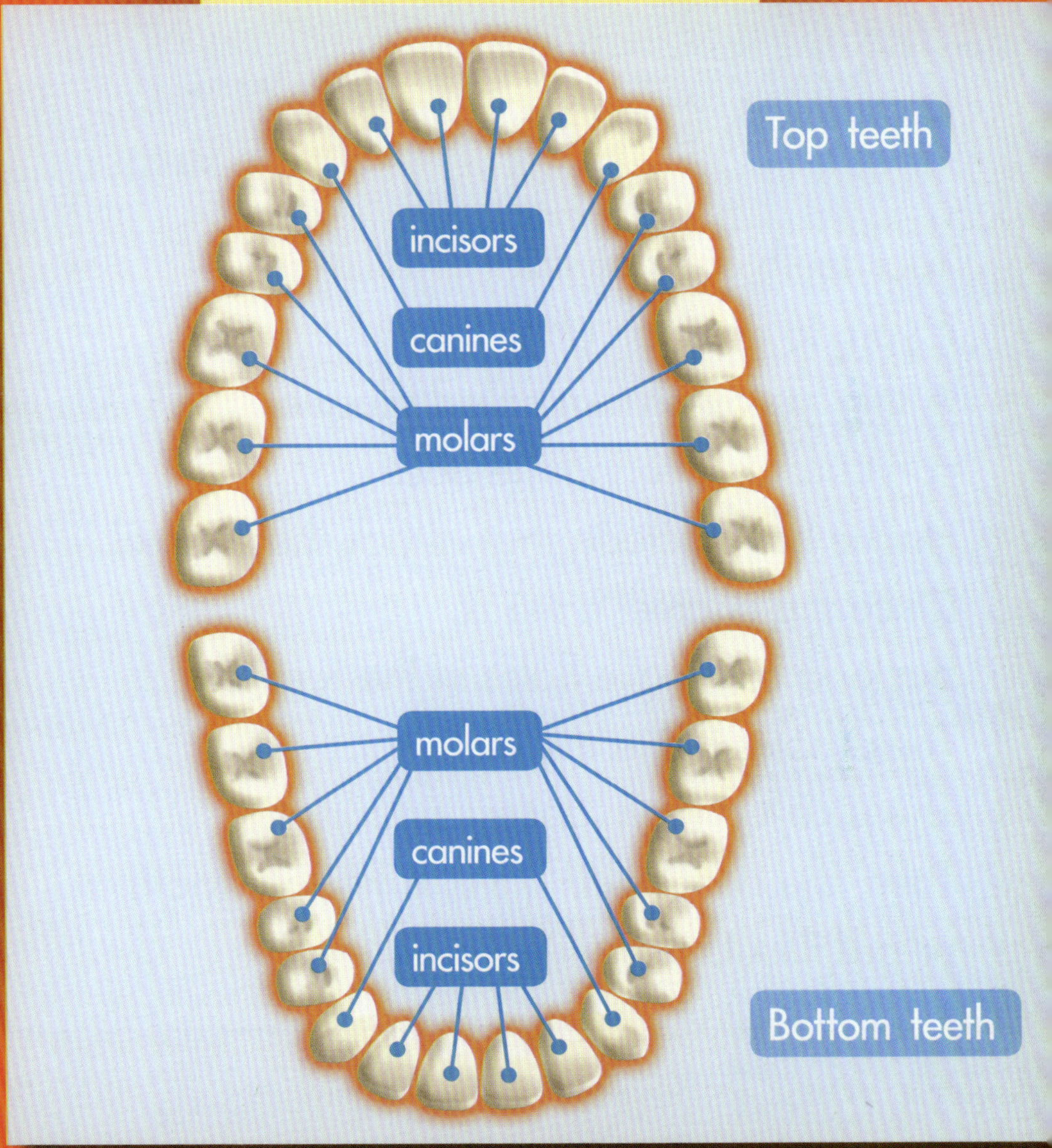

How Teeth Can Get Sick

Your teeth can get sick
if you do not look after them.
A thin, yellowish film called **plaque**
can build up around the base.
Plaque has bacteria that attack the enamel.
Once the enamel is weak,
bacteria can make holes in the teeth.
These holes make the teeth rot.
This is called tooth decay, or **caries**.
Then, the dentist will have to fill your tooth,
or pull it out.

The purple marks on this girl's teeth show where a dentist found plaque.

How to Keep Teeth Healthy

Cleaning your teeth keeps them healthy. Brush them with a fluoride toothpaste at least twice a day after meals. This helps prevent caries.

Brushing your teeth should be the last thing you do before you go to bed.

You should also clean between your teeth with dental floss.
Using dental floss will clean places that your toothbrush cannot reach.

Dental floss helps keep gums healthy.

Some foods are good for your teeth. Milk, yoghurt, and cheese have calcium, which makes your teeth strong. You should eat some calcium-rich foods every day.

Calcium-rich milk is good for teeth.

Foods and drinks that have a lot of sugar are bad for your teeth.
The bacteria in your mouth change the sugar into an acid that damages your teeth.

Eating a lot of sugary foods like this can damage your teeth.

And last but not least, go to the dentist often.
The dentist checks your teeth
and tells you how to look after them.

It is important to have a healthy mouth.

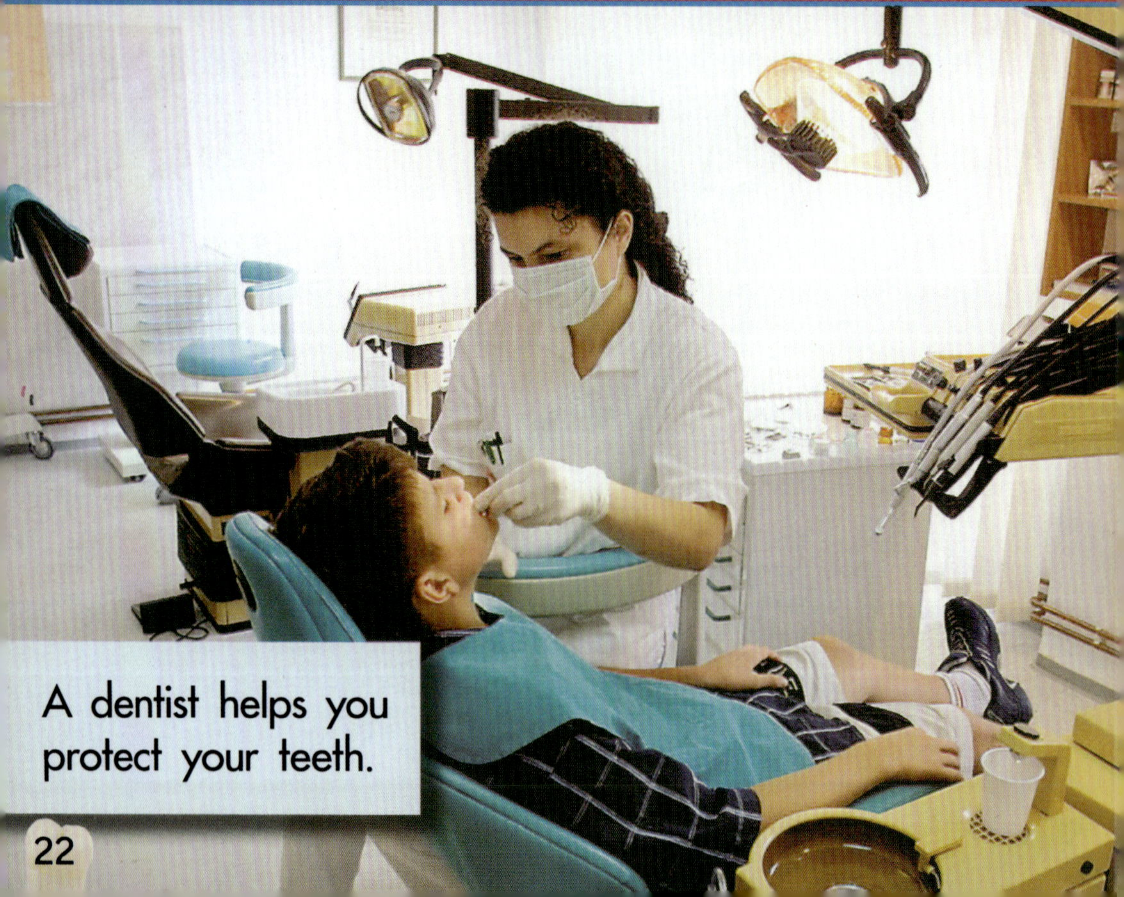

A dentist helps you protect your teeth.

Glossary

bacteria – very tiny living things that can make people sick

caries – tooth decay

enamel – the hard layer that covers the crown of a tooth

gums – the tissue around people's teeth

plaque – a yellowish film that builds up if people do not clean their teeth properly

saliva – the clear fluid in people's mouths

Index